How to teach this unit

For children to succeed in geography, they need to be able to relate the content to their lives; the curriculum must be relevant to them and fun to learn. Over the last few years Barnaby Bear, the lovable glove puppet, has helped bring geography to life for young children. Using the glove puppet and the wide range of Barnaby Bear big and little books, photographs, videos and artefacts, primary teachers have made geography fun for key stage 1 pupils: with Barnaby, children can visit places, and consider issues, far beyond the classroom.

Barnaby's capacity for travel is almost limitless: he goes on holiday with the children, of course, but also with the children's relatives, friends, teachers, school governors. Barnaby has his photograph taken in locations all over the world, and he sends postcards back to the class. Just like a six-year-old, Barnaby is full of wonder about the world – in the QCA unit, and in the wide range of published material, he visits many different localities and asks the sort of questions a naturally curious key stage 1 child would ask.

Geographical enquiry and skills covered by the unit include:

- asking key geographical enquiry questions (Where do oranges grow? What is the climate like where bananas grow?)

- observing and recording (visit to the supermarket)

- expressing their own views about people, places and environments (the use of packaging, for example)

- communicating in different ways (picture, speech, writing)

- using geographical vocabulary

- using fieldwork skills (recording information on the supermarket map)

- using globes, maps and plans at a variety of scales (to locate where food is grown)

- using secondary sources (CD-ROMS, the internet, reference books, pictures)

- making maps and plans (supermarket).

The **concept map** (page 7) illustrates how the QCA unit of work and this SuperSchemes unit can be developed over the year, to incorporate ongoing work about other localities and the use of the home and the local area.

What do I need to know?

This SuperSchemes unit makes use of Barnaby's immense educational potential to develop children's understanding of global interconnectedness and interdependence. The context is the child's own locality and home environment, and in this unit, the world comes to Barnaby Bear. It focuses on different foods and household items and how they come to us, demonstrating how the world enters all our homes every day. It has been designed to be inclusive and accessible to all key stage 1 pupils. Barnaby is a thinking, feeling, sensitive and reflective bear: this enables you to discuss with children what he might be thinking and feeling about the situations he finds himself in, and how they might react if they were in Barnaby's place.

Where do I start?

Explain to the children that this time Barnaby Bear is not travelling to a different place; instead, he is going to investigate how the world comes to him every day (see example lesson plan and medium term plan). You can use 'thinking skills' ideas and tasks to get the children really motivated, thinking and reflecting. Some very simple, but thought-provoking and creative, tasks are described on this page to support learning and teaching. Many of the ideas and tasks are generic and can be transferred to other areas of learning.

Time allocation

The teaching time available for geography can vary enormously. SuperSchemes units have been written with three possibilities in mind:

- a **short–medium** unit *(5–10 hours)*
- a **long** unit *(10–15 hours)*
- a **continuous** unit *(15–30 minutes per week)*

The medium term plans allow you to choose an appropriate length for your particular class. Some of the longer medium term plans offer enough material for you to continue with the topic later in the year.

Key ideas

Information and facts

Ask the children:

- to describe, in words and pictures, what happens on a banana/tea plantation
- to make an A–Z zigzag book reflecting how the world comes to Barnaby Bear each day
- to list, on two outline shopping bags, foods grown in the UK and foods grown in other countries
- to write instructions to explain to an alien how to shop in a supermarket.

Understanding

Ask the children:

- to describe, in diagrams and words, the procedure for shopping in a supermarket
- to write the instructions for making a healthy sandwich or a fresh fruit salad.

Feelings

Ask the children:

- How do you think Barnaby Bear would feel if there was no sugar grown in the world? What would he not be able to eat or drink? How would you feel?
- How do you think Barnaby Bear would feel if he got lost in a large supermarket? How would you feel? What should you do if you do get lost in a supermarket?

Strengths and weaknesses

Ask the children:

- How does a supermarket make it easier for Barnaby Bear's mum to do the family's shopping? Give the children two outline shopping trolleys and ask them to put the good points (advantages) in one and the bad points (disadvantages) in the other.
- Barnaby Bear's grandpa breaks his leg and has to use a wheelchair. How do supermarkets make it easier for disabled people to shop? Give the children two outline wheelchairs and ask them to fill one with the good points and the other with the bad points.

Creativity

Ask the children:

- to create a collage out of labels and adverts to represent a visit to a market or supermarket
- to develop music to reflect the sights, sounds and smells experienced in a market or supermarket.

Tasks using 'thinker's keys'

The Thinker's Keys activities listed here are based on the twenty Thinker's Keys first developed by Tony Ryan (Ryan, 1990). His Thinker's Keys were a set of twenty different activities designed to motivate and engage pupils in a wide range of thinking tasks. A range of question starters are presented as keys to unlocking pupils' analytical, critical and creative thinking abilities.

The reverse key

Name six things Barnaby would not be able to buy in a supermarket.

The 'what if?' key

What if we could only buy and eat items grown in the UK?

The alphabet key

Ask the children to make an A–Z zigzag book showing how the world comes to Barnaby Bear each day.

The different uses key

Find ten uses for:

- a tea bag
- a shopping trolley
- a coconut doormat.

The disadvantage key

List the disadvantages of shopping in a supermarket/over the internet, etc.

The alternative key

List all the ways Barnaby Bear's mum could buy her weekly groceries.

The brainstorming key

List all the different ways the world comes into your home each day (e.g. food, clothes and furniture, TV, e-mails, telephone, internet, newspapers, etc.)

Brainstorm ways to encourage people to buy more locally grown or fairly traded produce.

The question key

The answer is pure orange juice – what are five possible questions?

The answer is apple – what are five possible questions?

The answer is fair trade – what are five possible questions?

The predictions key

Predict three things that Barnaby would see in the supermarket but not at school, and three things he would see both in the supermarket and at school.

The construction key

Make a market stall out of waste material.

The interpretations key

Give three possible reasons why newspapers and magazines are sold in supermarkets.

The variations key

In how many different places can you buy a bunch of flowers, a newspaper, etc.?

The inventions key

Design a new type of healthy sandwich. Write the recipe. Make, eat and enjoy!

Medium term plan:

The world comes to Barnaby Bear!

Learning outcomes	Key questions	Pupil activities	Resources/ key vocabulary	Assessment opportunities
To understand that our own homes are linked to the wider world through the products used and eaten in our daily lives	How does the world come to Barnaby Bear's house every day?	■ Discuss reasons why Barnaby Bear is not at school and why he is not able to visit other places ■ Sequence the illustrations of a day in the life of Barnaby Bear (see **Activity 2**) ■ Use 'think, pair, share' strategy to discuss how the world comes to Barnaby Bear every day. List how what Barnaby Bear does and eats connects him with the rest of the world ■ Use **Activity sheet 1** to identify, name and discuss the item being used or eaten. Match this with where the item comes from (see **Example lesson plan**)	Illustrations of Barnaby Bear at home on CD (Activity 2) *Names of a range of food items found at home, e.g. milk, cakes, coffee, biscuits, etc*	Can children correctly sequence the illustrations and give good explanations and reasons for sequence? Can children correctly match food and its source?
To develop an understanding that different foods and materials are obtained from different places	Where in the world is … grown, made, assembled?	■ Make a class collection of labels from food packaging. Sort (categorise) under different headings. Present information using Venn diagrams ■ On a globe, find the places where different foods/goods come from ■ Make a class wall display and link the labels with the country of origin	Clean food packaging Globe Map of the world *Words appropriate for the chosen crop/product*	Can children sort the food labels and give good reasons for their categories? Are children able to discuss their work?
To develop an understanding that different foods are grown in different places because of different weather, climate, terrain To use a variety of sources.	Why are particular products grown in some places and not in others? How does the weather affect what is grown? Challenge question: How could bananas be grown in Iceland?	■ Investigate the conditions under which some products are grown ■ Using resources showing a tropical environment, discuss the weather there and the type of crops grown ■ Give the children in pairs a list of crops and ask them which are grown at home, which overseas and which in both places. Discuss their responses	Pictures of tropical environments List of fruit/vegetables *Words linked to crops discussed in class*	Can children link products to the climate correctly? Are they able to work together to make decisions? Do they demonstrate the ability to think creatively about the challenge question?
To identify where we get some of the necessities of life To understand that we do not all use the same facilities (e.g. local shops, greengrocers, fruit and vegetable market, supermarket, internet shopping, etc.)	What happens at a supermarket? Who puts things where? Which products are displayed together? Why? What are the hygiene implications? How are things packaged?	■ Fieldwork: Barnaby Bear visits a supermarket. Children to think of questions to guide discussion with manager ■ Use map of supermarket to locate … and to plan a route to buy …; use simple co-ordinates (see **Activity sheet 3**) ■ Compare and contrast supermarket with open-air fruit and vegetable market. Make a market stall ■ Buy items to make a fruit salad/healthy sandwich. Make and eat it.	Map of supermarket (**Activity sheet 3** on CD) *Range of words taken from the key on* **Activity sheet 3**; *market, stall, sandwich*	Can children devise suitable questions? Can they use a map to locate and plan a route? Are they able to discuss their work? Can they make a fruit salad/sandwich?
To start to develop views on packaging To develop an understanding of which materials can be recycled or reused, and how we can all contribute to keeping the environment tidy.	Is all the packaging necessary? How is the packaging disposed of/recycled? Does the supermarket have a recycling centre? Is there a problem with litter or people who do not take their trolleys back?	■ Investigate the packaging in a box of chocolate: individual wrappings, paper lining box, plastic moulded tray, etc. ■ How are things packaged? Make a collection of packaging. Sort packaging by: material, shape, size, re-usable/not re-usable, recyclable/non-recyclable ■ What happens to the rubbish? ■ In groups, make a sculpture out of waste, e.g. a fruit bowl out of old newspaper, to hold apples, bananas, oranges, etc.	Box of chocolates Clean food packaging Clean waste material, e.g. old newspaper *Range of words to do with packaging (plastic, paper, wrapping, tray) and recycling*	Can children sort material correctly? Can they discuss this? How well do they make models and sculptures? Can children say what the letters RRR stand for?

Cross-curricular links:

History; **Literacy** – lists, finding, selecting and recording information, communicating findings, speaking and listening; **ICT**; **Citizenship** – reducing waste, recycling rubbish, **RRR**; **Design** – design a market stall using boxes, art straws, dowelling, fabric, etc.; make a fruit salad or a sandwich; **Role play** – turn role play area into a market stall and link this with maths and numeracy (money).

Concept map

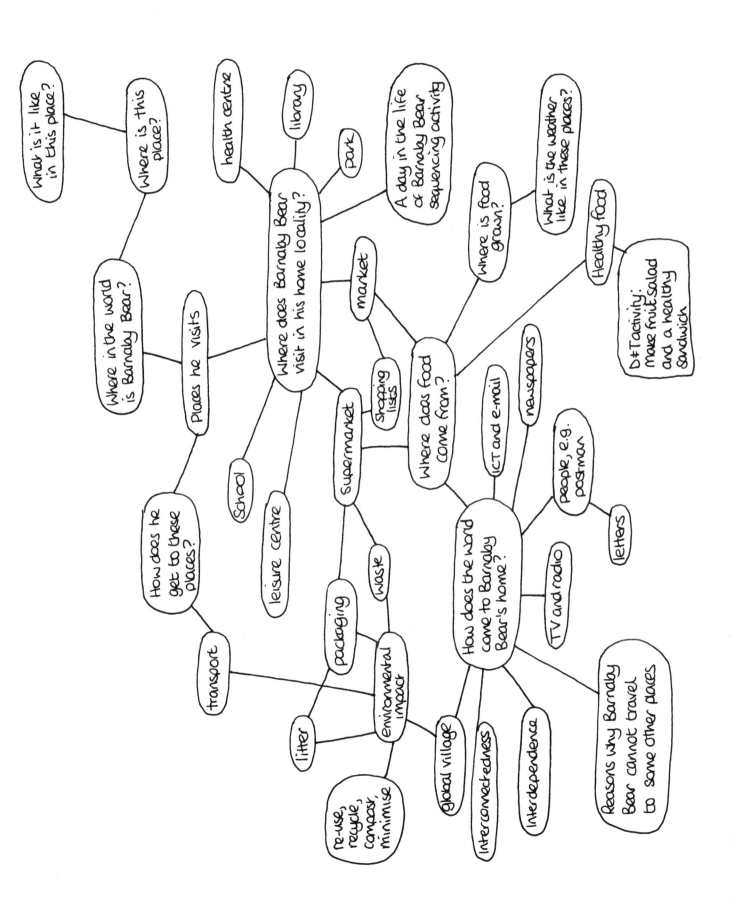

What is it like in this place?

Where is this place?

health centre

library

park

A day in the life of Barnaby Bear sequencing activity

What is the weather like in these places?

Where is food grown?

Healthy food

D&Tactivity: Make fruit salad and a healthy sandwich

Where in the world is Barnaby Bear?

Places he visits

Where does Barnaby Bear visit in his home locality?

market

Where does food come from?

ICT and e-mail

newspapers

People, e.g. postman

Shopping lists

Supermarket

School

leisure centre

waste

packaging

How does he get to these places?

transport

litter

environmental impact

re-use, recycle, compost, minimise

global village

How does the world come to Barnaby Bear's home?

TV and radio

letters

Interconnectedness

Interdependence

Reasons why Barnaby Bear cannot travel to some other places

Lesson plan:

How we're connected with the wider world

Subject: Geography (years 1-2)   **Time/Duration:** One hour 15 mins

Learning outcomes

In the lesson children will learn:

- that, like Barnaby Bear, their life and home are linked to the wider world through the food they eat and the products they use in their daily lives.

Background to the current lesson

This is the first lesson in a new unit of work. The children have previously investigated their school and immediate locality, and have very simple mapping skills.

Lesson details

Introduction

As whole class, discuss why Barnaby Bear might be absent from school (holiday, illness, etc.) and why he might be unable to visit other places (e.g. sickness, new baby in family, moving house, death in extended family, etc.). Focus on any reasons particularly relevant to this group of children. Link to PSHE. (10 minutes)

Main tasks

1. Group the children and give each group the seven illustrations of Barnaby (**Activity 2:** Barnaby Bear's day, from CD. This is a day when Barnaby does not leave home.) Ask them to discuss what Barnaby is doing in each illustration and then to sequence a day in his life. Teacher and LSA (if available) circulate round the groups, checking on the sequences, asking questions to deepen the discussion, and listening to the children's reasons for their decisions. (15 minutes)

2. Bring the whole class together. Recap the sequence of the illustrations. Pose the question: 'If Barnaby doesn't leave home, how does the world come to him?' Project each illustration onto a whiteboard and use 'think, pair, share' strategy to discuss how the world comes to Barnaby Bear – e.g. newspaper (paper from Canada), soap (oil palms from Asia), etc. As a whole class, make a list of what Barnaby Bear and his family eat and use, and where each product originated. TV, radio and the internet are also examples of how the world comes into our homes: news, weather, travel programmes, etc. (15 minutes)

3. Prepare **Activity Sheet 1**. If you can, display Photos 1-8 from the CD on the whiteboard. In twos and threes, grouped by ability, ask the children to identify and describe each item being used or eaten and then match it with its country of origin. Ask them to stick one picture of Barnaby in their

books, and write the name of the product and its country of origin. See **Differentiation** for development of this task. (30 minutes)

Plenary

- Bring the class together to share their work. Set the scene for the next lesson, including a visit to the supermarket. (5 minutes)

Differentiation (including use of LSA, if available)

For Task 1, the children are in mixed-ability groups.

For Task 3, the children are grouped by ability.

- **BA:** With initial support from LSA, complete **Activity Sheet 1**, then continue to match and stick pictures into books (each child will require a full set of cards).

- **A:** As a group, complete **Activity Sheet 1**, but without sticking pictures into books. Using a simple atlas and A3 outline world map, with appropriate countries named, locate countries where all the items are grown or produced. Stick the pictures of Barnaby on the appropriate place on the map. LSA to support when the children start to locate on map.

- **AA:** Complete **Activity Sheet 1**. Using the photographs, find two other items eaten or used by Barnaby's family and use simple reference books to find out where they come from. Discuss 'fair trade' in very simple terms. Teacher to support, especially for the research and discussion of fair trade.

Resources

Enough sets of Barnaby Bear's day (pictures 9-15) for all groups; IWB or projector screen; simple atlas or world map.

Simple A3 outline map, labelled with countries relevant to the task.

Enough copies of **Activity Sheet 1** for all the groups, cut into cards and shuffled.

Photos 1-8 from the CD.

Cross-curricular links

- Literacy – speaking and listening

- PSHE/Citizenship – why is Barnaby Bear staying at home?, fair trade, food miles, RRR (reduce, re-use, recycle).

Activity Sheet 1:

Where things come from

Further ideas for developing this unit

1 Human journeys

Learning objectives

Children develop an understanding that just like Barnaby, they make many different journeys, using different types of transport, in their own locality. Children develop an understanding of why different modes of transport are used for journeys of different length.

Tasks

As whole class, discuss the journeys Barnaby Bear and the children make in their own locality.

Ask the children to discuss in pairs:

- what journeys they think Barnaby might make in his own locality – to school, around home and school, to the library, health centre, local shops/supermarket, out-of-town shopping centre
- the different modes of transport – on foot, by bicycle, car, bus, train, tram, park and ride, etc.
- the different routeways he might use – footpaths, roads, railways.

Bring the ideas together as a whole class. These may become starting points for other units of work.

2 Food miles

Learning objectives

Children develop an understanding that food and other items they use in their daily lives may have been grown in a different country, and may have travelled thousands of miles before they reach their home. Children develop an understanding of why different modes of transport are used for different products and lengths of journey, and are able to identify similarities and differences between how some items are transported in various places.

Tasks

- How does … reach Barnaby Bear's home? What sort of transport is used to get … to Barnaby Bear's home? Ask the children to sequence journeys made by food items and other items 'from field to home', e.g. banana from plantation to shop, milk from cow to doorstep, cocoa from pod to chocolate bar, flowers from grower to home, etc.

- Link with Where are different foods grown? (below): how far do some items travel? As a class, discuss whether it is good to eat foods that have travelled so far, or whether it would be better if we ate locally grown and produced foods.

3 Where are different foods grown?

Learning objectives

Children develop an understanding that food and other items they use in their daily lives may have been grown in places where the climate and weather is very different from their own, and why they are grown there.

Tasks

- Make a class collection of labels from food packaging and adverts. Discuss each item – is it fruit, vegetable or meat? If fruit or vegetable, where does it grow – on trees, on bushes, in greenhouses, underground? Sort (categorise) items under different headings, e.g. foods grown and produced in the UK/outside the UK, foods grown in very hot countries/cooler climates, foods that are eaten raw/cooked and processed. Ask the children to present the information using Venn diagrams.

- On a globe or world map, find the places where the foods/goods come from. Make a class wall display and link the labels with the country of origin.

- In groups, using photographs and simple information texts, ask the children to find out about the climate and growing conditions of different foods or other items in daily use. What do the photographs and texts tell us about the landscape, soil, weather, people, etc.? Draw sketches and make notes. Report back to the whole class.

- Design and make different pizzas, with a different topping from a different country. Locate the countries on a world map.

4 Where do we buy our food?

Learning objective

Identify where and how we obtain some of the necessities of life. Children develop an understanding that we do not all use the same facilities, e.g. local shops, greengrocers, fruit and vegetable market, supermarket, etc. Children begin to develop an understanding of using co-ordinates and simple grid references to locate places.